H is for Hook

A Fishing Alphabet

Written by Judy Young and Illustrated by Gary Palmer

Sleeping Bear Press™

310 North Main Street, Suite 300
Chelsea, MI 48118
www.sleepingbearpress.com

© 2008 Sleeping Bear Press is an imprint of Gale, a part of Cengage Learning.

Printed and bound in China.

First Edition

10 9 8 7 6 5 4 3 2 1

Library of Congress Cataloging-in-Publication Data

Young, Judy.
H is for hook : a fishing alphabet / written by Judy Young;
illustrated by Gary Palmer.
p. cm.
Summary: "From A to Z all that is fishing is explained in this
illustrated picture book using poetry and prose. Topics include angler,
catch and release, fly-fishing, tackle, and more"—Provided by publisher.
ISBN 978-1-58536-347-6
1. Fishing—Juvenile literature. 2. English
language—Alphabet—Juvenile literature. I. Palmer, Gary, 1968- ill.
II. Title.
SH445.Y68 2008
799.1—dc22   2007034478

For Reid,
my favorite angler,
and with special thanks to
Capt. Mark Brown
for fishing trips aboard the Whole Life.

JUDY

§

For all the memories made wetting a hook with family and friends
at John and Faye Vick's pond, as well as Marion and Shirley Ross' pier.
Thanks for being patient.

GARY

Aa

A is for Angler
whose day is ideal
when he catches a fish
with a rod and a reel.

Have you ever gone fishing? Then you are an angler! An "angler" is a person who fishes with a hook and line. It comes from the Old English word "angul" that means "hook." Anglers come in all ages, can be male or female, and can live anywhere. Some anglers have lots of equipment. Others own only the basic necessities: a rod, reel, and hook.

People have been angling for thousands of years. During the Stone Age, lines made of sinew or plant fibers were tied to sticks. A sharp stone wrapped with bait was tied to the line. When a fish swallowed the bait, the stone caught in its throat, and the fish was pulled to shore. Later, hooks were carved from bones, then made from metal. Ancient Egyptian drawings show people fishing with rods and twelfth-century paintings from China show rods with reels.

Fishing for Facts: Today, fishing is the number one outdoor sport, with over 34 million licensed anglers in the United States and almost 4 million in Canada.

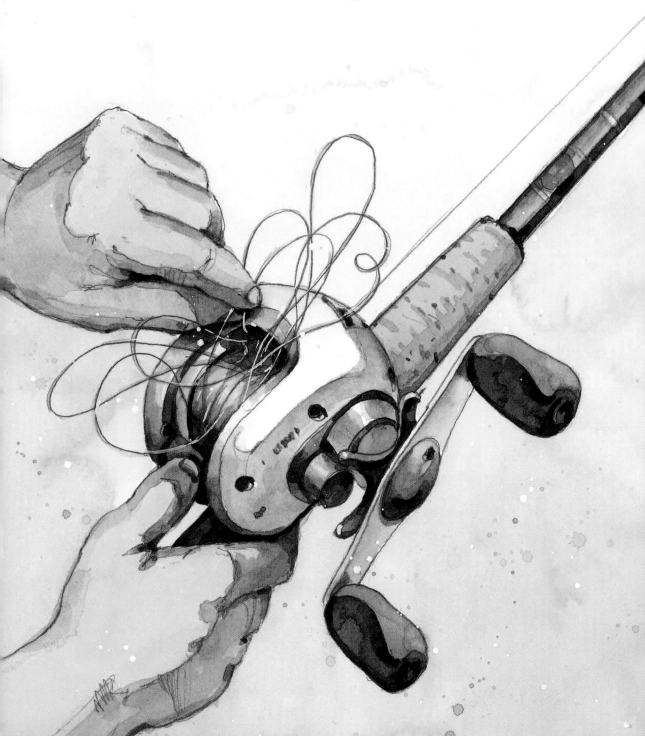

B is for Bird's Nest.
   Don't cry and don't pout.
Just patiently work
               'til the tangles are out.

Oh, no! A bird's nest! What a mess! Don't worry. Every angler gets the line tangled up some time. Try to gently untangle the line, but don't pull on it. That will only make it worse. If you can't get it straightened out, just cut off the tangle and tie the hook on again.

To tie on a hook, use a clinch knot. Practice tying knots at home so you'll know how when you go fishing. Here's how:

1. Thread about six inches of line through the hook's eye.
2. Wrap this "tag" end around the main line five times.
3. Look. There's a space between the hook and the wrapped line. Thread the end through it.
4. Now, it's made another loop under the wrapped line. Put the end through it, too.
5. Hold the hook and wrapped line between your thumb and finger.
6. Steadily pull the main line with your other hand to tighten the knot.
7. Trim off the end.

Fishing for Facts: Fishing line is hazardous to animals. Throw bird's nests in the trash.

Bb

Catch a fish and let it go.
It helps populations increase.
Fish will be there another day
when C is for Catch and Release!

C c

Many anglers choose to "catch and release" fish. In some places laws require fish to be returned to the water. Released fish can be caught again, plus they can grow and produce more fish, assuring healthy fish populations.

To help fish survive being caught, use barbless hooks. They don't have the sharp point sticking out in the opposite direction from the main point, so they're easier to remove without harming the fish. If you can't get the hook out, either cut the hook where it bends, or cut the line. The hook will rust away. It's best to release a fish without taking it from the water. But if you take it out, wet your hands before handling it so you won't damage its scales. Also, limit the time it's out of water. Finally, when releasing the fish, don't drop or throw it. Glide it gently back into the water.

Fishing for Facts: To help fish populations, the United States has 69 National Fish Hatcheries that raise over 100 species of fish.

Some fish eat just about anything; others are very picky. In order to catch specific kinds of fish, you need to know what they like for dinner! Some fish will eat things you eat, such as bread, cheese, hot dogs, corn, and even marshmallows! Many fish prefer worms or insects such as grasshoppers and crickets. Frogs, crawdads, and salamanders make a delicious dinner for some freshwater species and saltwater fish love shrimp, squid, and crabs. In fresh and salt water, however, many fish eat other fish.

Anglers may choose to fish with live bait, a fish's most natural diet. Sometimes, anglers use natural bait that has been frozen. Natural bait cut into bite-size chunks is called cut bait. You can dig worms, catch grasshoppers, or seine for minnows yourself, or you can buy live or frozen bait at a tackle shop or marina.

Fishing for Facts: Game fish are species anglers try to catch. Baitfishes are species fishermen use as bait but do not try to catch with a rod and reel.

Minnows, mayflies, beetles, bugs,
a great big mullet, a small sandflea,
larvae, leeches, night crawlers, nymphs—
Dinner is for the letter D.

D d

Fish fries, fritters, casseroles,
fish with sauces, sour and sweet,
gumbos, chowders, fish kabobs—
letter E means fish to Eat.

Fish are delicious to eat. They can be cooked many ways, but before cooking a fish it must be cleaned. You don't clean a fish with soap and water. Cleaning a fish means getting it ready to cook. To clean a fish, the belly is cut open and the internal organs removed. With some fish, such as trout, this is all you do before cooking. With most fish, however, you remove the head, tail, and dorsal fin, and also scrape off the scales before cooking. Be careful when eating; there may be small bones.

Another way to prepare a fish for cooking is to *fillet* (fil-LAY) it. When filleted, the meat is cut away from the back and rib bones, and the skin is removed, leaving a nice piece of boneless meat, ready for your favorite recipe.

Fishing for Facts: While cleaning fish, become a forensic scientist! Look in the fish's stomach to see what it had been eating. Keep this in mind the next time you select bait or lures.

William Shakespeare wrote, "A trout... must be caught with tickling," and that is what the fly-fisherman attempts to do—tickle the fish's attention through the presentation of a fly. With fly-fishing, lures called "flies" are made by tying feathers, fur, tinsel, wool, and other materials onto hooks. Many flies imitate insects, and the angler tries to match what is hatching at the moment. Other flies look like insect larvae, minnows, crabs, or worms. Often anglers enjoy tying their own flies. "Dry flies" are tied so they float on the surface; "wet flies" sink.

Special rods and reels, as well as special tapered line, are used for fly-fishing. It takes a lot of practice to learn to cast with a fly rod. By moving the rod back and forth, the line loops and rolls through the air, until it lengthens out to land the fly on the water. The movement and weight of the line carries the fly to the perfect spot.

Fishing for Facts: Some flies are smaller than $1/16$th of an inch.

When F is for Fly-fishing
the line loops and rolls
to deliver a fly
to the fish in the holes.

F f

All fish have to breathe
just like you and me.
But how does a fish accomplish this?
With Gills! They're for letter G!

G g

All fish have gills. To breathe, a fish takes water into its mouth and pushes it through its gills. There, oxygen is removed from the water and enters the fish's bloodstream. Then the water is pushed out through gill slits behind the fish's eyes.

Fish also have fins, which help them move. A fish swims by twisting its body from side to side like an "S," pushing the water with its tail to give it power. Top and bottom fins give the fish balance and side fins help it start, stop, and turn. An air-filled swim bladder under a fish's backbone keeps the fish from sinking to the bottom.

Most fish have scales that protect the skin. Slime coats the scales, helping the fish swim faster and protecting it from disease. A sense organ called a lateral line, which runs from the gills to the base of the tail, lets the fish feel vibrations.

Fishing for Facts: Nearly all fish are cold-blooded. Their body temperature is determined by the water temperature.

To find where fish hide, think like a fish! Fish like to eat, but they are lazy. Fish are afraid of predators and they don't like the sun.

So you'll find fish in places where the current carries dinner right to them, such as near eddies, on the outside edges of river bends, in pools below waterfalls, and where waters from two streams merge. Fish rest in calmer pockets that form downstream behind boulders so they don't have to fight rushing water. They hide under ledges and rocks, around sunken trees, or in vegetation, where they feel safer from bigger fish, birds, and mammals. Fish hang out in shady spots under overhanging trees, bushes, and docks. They go deeper as the day heats up, liking the cooler water in deep holes, against steep banks or near springs. Fish often eat in the morning or evening, when it's cooler.

Fishing for Facts: If you catch a fish from a good spot, another will take his place, so fish that spot again next time!

H h

H is for Hiding
'cause that's what fish do,
    under logs and stone ledges
    and in grasses, too.

Button your coat;
put your warm mittens on.
I is for Ice fishing
on a cold, frozen pond.

Do you live where it gets really cold in the winter? You could go ice fishing! When ice on a lake is about five inches thick, ice fishermen bundle up in their warmest clothes, walk out onto a frozen lake and drill holes in the ice with an auger. Using short rods, they drop weighted lines into the holes, jigging either live bait or artificial lures close to the bottom until a fish bites. Some ice fishermen don't use a rod. Their lines are hooked to special contraptions called "tip-ups." When a fish bites, a flag tips up to let them know to pull in the line.

Many ice fishermen sit in special tents they put up around their fishing holes. Some drive vehicles across the frozen lake, pulling small shacks over their fishing holes. These shacks are often heated with wood or gas stoves, and may even have electricity!

Fishing for Facts: Walking on frozen lakes, ponds, and rivers is dangerous. Never go out on the ice without an adult's permission.

I i

Did you have a fantastic day of fishing? Write about it in a journal! Many anglers record what has been successful to help improve chances of having another good catch.

Start your journal entry with the date and specific location such as "James River near McGraw's Ford." Include conditions such as time (dawn, morning, afternoon, dusk), temperature (hot, warm, chilly, cold), weather (clear, overcast, drizzly, raining, snowing) and water level (high, low, average).

Now for the fish! Record not only the kind and size of fish you caught, but where and how you caught them. Did you catch your big bass near a bank or beside a sunken tree? What kind and size of bait did you use? What kind and color of lure? Did you fish the surface or deep? Did you reel in quickly or slowly jig the line?

Fishing for Facts: Be observant! The more aware you are about when, where, and what the fish are biting, the better angler you will be.

Jj

Exactly when, what, where, and how
I caught a bunch of fish today,
is what I'll write when day is done;
My Journal is for letter J.

You've hauled in your fish, but is it a keeper? There are laws about which fish can be kept. Size regulations say fish must be at least or no longer than a certain length. Catch limits tell how many fish of a certain species can be kept. Some species cannot be kept at all and must be released. Some fishing locations may have specific regulations such as fly-fishing only. Fishing "seasons" prohibit fishing certain times of the year. This protects fish during spawning when they lay eggs.

Laws differ from place to place and species to species. In most states and provinces, children under 16 do not need a fishing license, but it is up to any aged angler to know and follow the regulations. Anglers can get rulebooks wherever fishing licenses are sold. Fish identification books help anglers learn what kind of fish they catch.

Fishing for Facts: Keep keepers cold, either in water using a stringer or a wire fish basket, or in a cooler on ice.

You've measured each fish
on your stringer today.
Caught your limit of Keepers:
Wow! That's letter K.

L is for Lure—
a jig, spoon, or spinner—
that tricks a fish
into thinking it's dinner.

Lures are artificial bait designed to imitate the way a fish's natural food looks, moves, sounds, and even smells. Thousands of different lures are made from variations of five basic types: plugs, spoons, spinners, jigs, and plastic worms.

Plugs look like fish. Surface plugs swim across the top of the water. Floating-diving plugs do just that: float, then dive when you reel. Deep plugs have long bills. The longer the bill, the deeper they go when reeled. Spoons are curved pieces of metal that flash, resembling shiny baitfish. Spinners have metal disks that rotate rapidly, fluttering and sparkling like baitfish. Jigs are hooks with weights that look like heads. Colored feathers or shimmering tinsel attached to the jig will attract a fish. When reeling in a jig, jerk the line slightly so it dances and darts through the water in spurts. Plastic worms squiggle and squirm, looking like a live worm when reeled.

Fishing for Facts: Bigger isn't always better! You can catch a big fish on a tiny lure.

L1

Not only is it fun to fish, but memories of fishing are also fun. Nothing is better than sitting around with fellow anglers and swapping fish stories. Every angler loves to talk about the "big one that got away," as well as the one landed, how it fought, and how it was outsmarted. Many fish stories stretch the imagination with humorous exaggeration and everyone who has ever wet a line has a story to contribute.

Looking at photographs from fishing trips also brings up memories of good times and good people. Do you have a picture of the first fish you caught? Hey! Is that your lucky hat in that picture? Or is that the hat that floated away when you leaned over to net your big keeper? Look! There's Uncle Bob kissing his fish! Remember that? It was a fun day!

Fishing for *Fiction*: "Lord, give me grace to catch a fish so big that even I, when talking about it afterward, shall have no cause to lie." Anonymous

M
m

M is for the Memories
we love to share with friends.
And when we tell our fishing tales
the laughter never ends.

Your fish is tired out, and you've pulled him up close. He's a big one! How are you going to land him? Grab the net!

If you have a big fish, or you're in a boat, you may want to net your fish. Wait until the fish has stopped fighting aggressively. Don't swipe at the fish with the net, but completely submerge the net in the water. Gently pull the fish toward the net. Bringing the net underneath the fish, scoop it up headfirst. It sounds simple but if you don't keep your rod tip up, your line may lose tension and the fish may spit the hook. Or you may knock the fish with the net's rim and the fish will escape. If the fish sees the net, he may take another run, so don't set your rod down before he's landed.

Fishing for Facts: Fish can also be landed by grabbing the lower lip with your finger and thumb. Beware: some fish have teeth! Ouch!

You had a strike;
your hook was set;
you've brought him in.
Now N is for Net.

I've got a marlin on my line—
a thousand pounds of fish, or more!
I hooked him in the ocean deep
where O is for fishing way Offshore!

If you go offshore where land is far from sight, you may catch a wahoo, a tuna, maybe even a shark! Offshore anglers dream of fighting giant billfish like marlin and sailfish.

How can you find fish in a great big ocean? Maps and special equipment point out rocks, ledges, and wrecks where fish hang out deep underwater. Fish also hide under free-floating objects, weed lines, and near oil rigs where there is shade. Anglers "chum" the water, tossing a chopped-up baitfish stew overboard. Fish are attracted to the smell.

Once a large fish bites, it may take hours to pull it in. Anglers may be strapped into chairs bolted to the boat while they fight their huge fish. A big hook attached to a pole, called a gaff, is used to haul the fish into the boat, but some anglers photograph and release their catch.

Fishing for Facts: Watch the birds! Gulls and terns often tell saltwater anglers where bait-fishes are, and bigger fish may be nearby.

Oo

Pp

Patient, Persistent,
and Polite start with P.
You'll have a great day
if you are all three!

When you go fishing, you must be patient and persistent. Every angler knows you won't get a bite with every cast and some days you aren't going to catch any fish at all. However, you won't catch a fish with your line out of water, so keep trying.

Fishing isn't only about catching fish. Fishing can be a relaxing, quiet time to think or an opportunity to enjoy a buddy's company. It's also a chance to enjoy being outdoors. You might see a duck flying overhead, a turtle sunning himself, or an iridescent dragonfly hovering over the water. Maybe a deer or fox will come for a drink.

Fishing will be pleasant for everyone if you are polite. If someone is already fishing in a certain spot, don't crowd him. Move to another place. Don't cast over someone else's line and if someone near you hooks a fish, reel in, so his fish won't get tangled up in your line.

Fishing for Facts: Be polite to the environment, too. Don't litter.

Shhhhhh! If you want to catch fish, you must be quiet. Sound travels easily through water and fish have excellent hearing. Noises made by stomping loudly on shore or by dropping items on the floor of a boat may scare fish away. Fish have good vision, too. If you can see a fish, it can see you. Movement may spook a fish, so sneak up on a fishing hole and don't wear bright colors.

Fish can also sense vibrations and may be frightened if you splash or throw things in the water. However, a fish's ability to detect vibrations can also help you catch it. Some vibrations drive a fish crazy, thinking dinner is swimming near. Moving your lure through the water to make similar vibrations can entice a fish to strike. Be patient. It takes practice to learn how to move different lures to trick a fish.

Fishing for Facts: Sound travels through water at over 3,000 m.p.h. That's about four times faster than through air.

Q

q

Q is for very Quiet,
    which is what you need to be.
So, sneak up to your fishing hole
    'cause fish can hear and fish can see.

R is for a Rod and Reel
so you can cast for fish.
And maybe in that big long box
you'll find your birthday wish!

R
r

A "fishing pole" is called a rod. Rods come in many lengths and weights, depending on what kind of fish you are after and the type of reel you have. They are usually made from fiberglass or graphite, have a handgrip, a reel seat to hold the reel, and round guides through which the line is threaded.

Reels hold, release, and retrieve the line. Closed-face spincasting reels are good for beginners. They rarely tangle and are easily operated by pushing a button. A spinning reel casts farther, but remembering to flip the bail and hold the line with a finger makes it trickier to use. A baitcasting reel holds heavier line for big fish. Difficult to cast, it will backlash into a big tangle if you don't remember to "thumb" the spool.

Fishing for Facts: The reel's "drag" controls how easily a fish can take out line. With too little drag, there's not enough pressure and the fish may spit the hook. Too much drag and the fish might break the line.

S is for Safety.
That's rule number one!
Those who fish safely
are those who have fun!

It's fun to fish, but it is important to be safe!

- Learn how to swim and always wear a life jacket.
- Fish with a buddy, and tell someone where you are going and when you will be back.
- Be careful: rocks, logs, banks, docks, etc. may be slippery.
- Don't wade unless you are with an adult.
- When wading, feel the bottom with your feet for drop-offs before stepping.
- Don't wade in fast or deep water.
- Make sure nobody is behind you before casting.
- Be careful handling fish. Some bite and some have poisonous barbs.
- Don't go barefoot. You may step on a hook or sharp rock.
- Watch the weather. If you hear thunder, stop fishing and seek shelter.

Fishing for Facts: Remember, all the fun of fishing disappears if someone gets hurt.

Ss

Leaders, sinkers, bobbers, hooks,
a spool of line, a tiny weight,
when Tackle is for letter T
you make a rig to hold your bait.

When you open a tackle box you may recognize hooks, but what's all that other stuff? Tackle is fishing equipment.

Bobbers are floats. They hold the bait at the depth you want. When a fish nibbles at the bait, the bobber wiggles. When the fish strikes, the bobber goes completely under! Sinkers are weights. A common type, the split shot sinker, is pinched around your line. Use just enough weight to pull the hook down without pulling the bobber under. Without bobbers, sinkers pull bait down deep to bottom fish. Swivels keep your line from twisting. Some snap open so you can quickly change lures without having to tie a knot. Leaders are short pieces of line tied between other pieces of tackle. By combining bobbers, sinkers, swivels, leaders, and hooks, you make a rig. Be creative and see what works!

A well-stocked tackle box may also include lures, line, pliers, knives, and hook removers.

Fishing for Facts: Hook size numbers seem backward. The smaller the hook, the bigger the number.

U is for Urban fishing
   in your town or in mine.
With buildings in the background,
   Let's go wet a line!

You don't have to take a trip to the country to go fishing. Many urban areas have wonderful places to cast a line! Steelheads can be caught in the Grand River where it runs through Grand Rapids, Michigan. Do you have a river or creek running through your city or town? Hundreds of lakes dot Minneapolis, Minnesota. Maybe there's a lake in your cityscape. Does your neighborhood park have a fishing pond stocked full of fish? One in Rolla, Missouri, does! If you live near salt water, like those in Camp Ellis, Maine; Port Mansfield, Texas; or Vancouver, British Columbia; there may be jetties or piers where fishing is allowed. Scout out your favorite urban fishing hole!

Many states and provinces have urban fishing programs. Towns and cities often have fishing clubs, classes, competitions, and festivals as well. Some are just for kids!

Fishing for Facts: The first full week of June is National Fishing Week in the United States, and in Canada, it's the first week of July!

U u

There are over 80 varieties of freshwater fish in North America that anglers love to land.

Largemouth and smallmouth bass are predators that eat almost anything. When they strike, they strike hard. Largemouth bass tend to go after fast-moving lures. Smallmouth bass chase slower lures that twitch and pause. Bluegills, pumpkinseeds, sunfish, rock bass (goggle eye), crappie, and perch are referred to as "panfish" because they are just the right size for a frying pan. Panfish will strike about any small bait or lure. Although easy to catch, they put up a strong fight for their small size.

Catfish and walleye are bottom feeders, so fish deep. Muskies and pike fiercely attack shiny, noisy surface bait. Rainbows, steelheads, cutthroat, brook trout, and brown trout are some of the most prized catches. These fast fish are picky eaters but love small insects and are fun to catch fly-fishing. Reeling in a lake trout or salmon is also an angler's dream.

Fishing for Facts: There are over 25,000 species of fish in the world.

A bluegill, bass, and catfish, too,
strung on my stringer, one, two, three!
So many fish that I can catch
when Variety is for letter V.

Some fish like it very cold,
    others like it hotter.
    But fish will always be around
when W is for Water!

Everyone knows fish live in water but good anglers know just what kind of water! Some fish live in freshwater creeks, rivers, ponds, or lakes; others in salty oceans. If you want to catch trout, you must fish places with very cold water, like spring-fed rivers or mountain lakes. Bass, however, like warmer waters. Walleye and catfish hang out in deep water. Pike can be found in shallower waters.

Anglers also fish from many places. Some cast from a riverbank or the shoreline of a pond or lake. Others relax on a dock with their hook, line, and sinker dropped over the side. Many anglers wade-fish shallow waters of streams and, at the ocean, surf-casting into the waves is fun. Boats allow anglers to go where the fish are. The boat may be anchored or you might drift-fish, floating with the current. Pulling a line slowly through the water with a motorboat is called trolling.

Fishing for Facts: Wherever you fish, follow safety rules and get permission to go on private property.

The letter **X** marks the spot
in the middle of your backyard.
If you practice it at home
casting won't be very hard!

To get your lure to the fish, you must learn how to cast accurately. You don't have to practice in water, though. Try lawn casting! Set up a target in your yard or a park. A towel or piece of cardboard will work. Tie a practice lure with no hooks onto your line. Now, stand about five giant steps from your target.

Imagine a clock with you in the middle and 12:00 above your head. Hold in the button on your reel with your thumb. Keeping your elbow bent and near your side, bring your hand up by your head until the tip of your rod goes back to about 10:00. Smoothly, flick your rod forward, stopping when the tip reaches 2:00. As you move your rod forward, let your thumb off the button. Your line will fly in the direction your rod tip is pointing. If you hit the target, back up five more steps and try again!

Fishing for Facts: Hitting the target is more important than how far you can cast.

Y y

Catching a fish of any size is exciting and calls for a "yippee!" and "yahoo!" Yet, every angler dreams of catching "the big one!" The size of a "big one" depends on the species. A two-pound sunfish is close to a record but is tiny compared to the record 1,805-pound blue marlin!

Where you catch a fish also makes a difference in determining if it is a "lunker." A one-pound brook trout would be an amazing catch from a shallow mountain stream, but from the much larger Nipigon River in Ontario, the world-record brookie was 14 pounds, 8 ounces. Fish in southern waters also tend to be bigger than the same species in northern waters. A largemouth bass caught in Ontario in 1976 weighed in at 10 pounds, 4 ounces, making it a Canadian record, but a 22 pound, 4 ounce largemouth caught in Georgia in 1932 is the U.S. record.

Fishing for Facts: Check out your state's or province's record catches, often listed in regulation handbooks or Web sites.

Y is for Yelling
Yippee and Yahoo!
When you catch a big fish,
that's what you do!

Z is for a big long Zzzzzzzzzing!
To anglers, this sounds so divine,
for when the reel starts to sing,
a great big fish is on the line!

You open your tackle box and choose your favorite lure, the chartreuse one. Looking across the water, you eye the perfect spot. In a fluid motion, you set your lure sailing. Plop! A perfect cast! You reel in your line, not too quickly, not too slowly, then cast it out again. Patiently, you reel in and cast out, over and over. You notice a bird on long stilted legs. He's fishing, too.

Suddenly, there's a tug on your line! You've got a bite! You snap your rod back, setting the hook. Zzzzzzzzzzzzzzzzzing! The sound every angler loves to hear: the fish pulling out line! Thump, thump, thump, your heart beats with excitement! The fish slows down, and you start to reel, smooth and steady. Wait! Don't force him! Zzzzzzzzzzzzzzzzzing! He's taking another run! Here we go again! What a fight! The fish finally tires out and you proudly pull him from the water. Snap! Your buddy's camera catches you and your fish!

Fishing for Facts: Grab your rod. The fish are waiting!

Z
z

Judy Young

Judy Young loves to fish! She's caught speckled sea trout and redfish in the Laguna Madre, snapper, king-fish, and sharks in the Gulf of Mexico, trout in mountain streams of Colorado and Idaho, and many other species in Missouri where she lives with her husband, Ross.

Judy thinks writing is like fishing. You bait your mind with an idea and cast it out to attract other ideas. Soon, you get a bite and reel in a keeper to write down. Judy helps students "fish for poems" by visiting schools with her poetry writing workshops. She has written four other "keepers" for Sleeping Bear Press: *Lazy Days of Summer*, *R is for Rhyme: A Poetry Alphabet*, *S is for Show Me: A Missouri Alphabet*, and *Show Me the Number: A Missouri Number Book*. Visit Judy at www.judyyoungpoetry.com.

Gary Palmer

Gary Palmer began showing an interest in drawing as early as five years of age. While residing in Key West, Florida with his family, he began painting scenes on driftwood and selling them to the local tourist shops. From those meager beginnings, Gary has pursued a successful career in illustration.

After attending the Ringling School of Art in Sarasota, Florida, Gary moved to North Carolina with his wife, Rebecca. They have two sons, Joel and Evan. Gary's illustrations have appeared in national advertising campaigns, magazines, and corporate promotions. He has illustrated murals for museums, promotions for zoos, and prints for a nature conservancy. *H is for Hook: A Fishing Alphabet* is Gary's fourth book with Sleeping Bear Press, and another opportunity to get out and explore his own passion for fishing.